AF270664

Barbie in the 1990s

DiscoverRoo
An Imprint of Pop!
popbooksonline.com

by Elizabeth Andrews

popbooksonline.com/nineties

abdobooks.com

Published by Pop!, a division of ABDO, PO Box 398166, Minneapolis, Minnesota 55439. Copyright © 2025 by Abdo Consulting Group, Inc. International copyrights reserved in all countries. No part of this book may be reproduced in any form without written permission from the publisher. DiscoverRoo™ is a trademark and logo of Pop!.

Printed in the United States of America, North Mankato, Minnesota.
052024
082024

THIS BOOK CONTAINS RECYCLED MATERIALS

Cover Photo: MATTEL/SIPA/Newscom

Interior Photos: Getty Images, Shutterstock Images, Design Bay Productions, Splash News/Mattel/Newscom, lil'_wiz/flickr, Alamy Stock Photo, MATTEL/SIPA/Newscom, WARNER BROTHERS/Album/Newscom

Editor: Grace Hansen

Series Designer: Victoria Bates

Library of Congress Control Number: 2023947577

Publisher's Cataloging-in-Publication Data

Names: Andrews, Elizabeth, author.

Title: Barbie in the 1990s / by Elizabeth Andrews

Description: Minneapolis, Minnesota : Pop!, 2025 | Series: Barbie through the decades | Includes online resources and index

Identifiers: ISBN 9781098246280 (lib. bdg.) | ISBN 9781098246846 (ebook)

Subjects: LCSH: Barbie dolls--Juvenile literature. | Toys--History--Juvenile literature. | Nineteen nineties--Juvenile literature. | Toys--Social aspects--Juvenile literature. | Popular Culture--Juvenile literature.

Classification: DDC 688.722--dc23

*Scanning QR codes requires a web-enabled smart device with a QR code reader app and a camera.

TABLE OF Contents

CHAPTER 1
Barbie's Beginnings. 4

CHAPTER 2
Living in the Real World 10

CHAPTER 3
Nineties Barbie Fashion 16

CHAPTER 4
Barbie Gets Real. 22

Making Connections. 30
Glossary 31
Index. 32
Online Resources 32

Barbie's Beginnings

Humans have made dolls for thousands of years. At first, dolls were made of clay, straw, or other natural materials. As the world changed, so did dolls. The toys got more detailed and exciting. In 1959, the fashion doll, Barbie, hit store shelves. The doll game was never the same.

Barbie's original striped swimsuit was inspired by fashions worn in the 1950s.

Ruth Handler was the creator of Barbie. Ruth and her husband owned the toy company Mattel Creations. Ruth noticed that children's dolls were mostly baby dolls. She believed growing girls didn't want to play with babies. They wanted dolls that encouraged them to dream of their futures.

Ruth Handler was born in Denver, Colorado, in 1916.

Mattel released the first Barbie in 1959. She wore a black-and-white swimsuit, black high heels, white sunglasses, and gold earrings. Barbie was a teenage fashion model from Willows, Wisconsin. She cost $3. Her extra outfits ranged between $1 and $5.

The Handler family

Barbie's full name is Barbara Millicent Roberts. She was named after Ruth's daughter Barbara.

Barbie was a hit! In the first year, Mattel sold 350,000 dolls. Soon customers were asking for more. Mattel went on to create friends, dreamhouses, cars, and more than 250 careers for Barbie. Ruth was right. Children did like grown-up dolls. Their imaginations grew with Barbie!

The first Barbie appeared passive and gentle. She fit into the late 1950s female tradition of **homemaking** and beauty **trends**. Some of the first Barbies included Barbie Learns to Cook and Suburban Shopper Barbie. However, Ruth wouldn't keep Barbie in the home for long.

Suburban Shopper Barbie, 1959

CHAPTER 2

Living in the Real World

The 1990s were a peaceful and **prosperous** time for Americans. Most people were living in cities and **suburbs**. Families often had two incomes per household as both men and women had careers. They had more money to spend and exciting things to spend it on!

The Mall of America was a new and exciting destination that opened in 1992. People could shop and even visit an amusement park.

Though women remained the main caretakers at home during the nineties, they were also taking the lead in the workforce. Many women ran for political office in the 1990s. In fact, 1992 came to be known as the "Year of the Woman."

From left to right, Senators Dianne Feinstein, Carol Moseley Braun, Barbara Mikulski (behind), Patty Murray, and Barbara Boxer.

Feinstein was a senator until she passed away at the age of 90.

More women than ever before won their elections! The number of women in **Congress** increased by three times in 1992. Barbara Boxer and Dianne Feinstein were elected to office in California. Carol Moseley Braun won her election, becoming the first Black woman in the Senate.

The digital age was born in the nineties. Science and technology advanced faster than ever before. The World Wide Web went public and people everywhere could use the Internet. By the late 1990s online businesses, such as eBay, were common. Video games, television, and movies advanced as well.

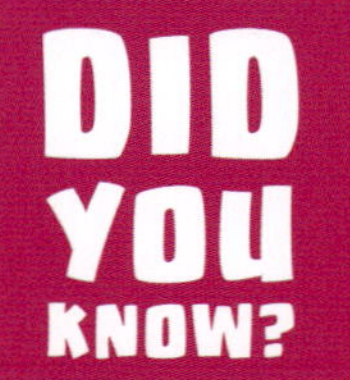

DID YOU KNOW?

The Women's National Basketball Association (WNBA) debuted in 1997.

America dominated the sports world throughout the nineties. The United States Women's National Team (USWNT) won the first ever Women's World Cup in 1991. In 1992, the US Men's Olympic Basketball Team won gold. They were called the Dream Team because the roster included basketball legends Michael Jordan, Larry Bird, Magic Johnson, and Charles Barkley.

The USWNT beat Norway in the World Cup championship.

15

CHAPTER 3

Nineties Barbie Fashion

In 1992, Totally Hair Barbie hit the shelves. Barbie's long-crimped hair reached all the way to her toes. She came with ribbons and bows for children to play at **styling** her long locks. Dressed in a bright colored minidress and bold accessories, Totally Hair Barbie fit early '90s **trends**.

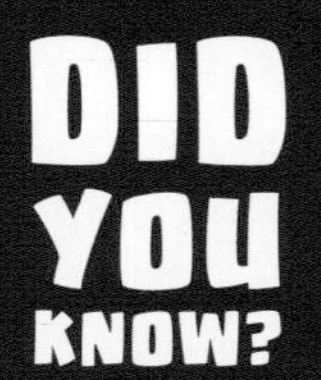

Totally Hair Barbie is the best-selling Barbie doll of all time.

Totally Hair Barbie, 1992

Shopping Malls

The mall was the place to be for people in the 1990s. Young people could go and hang out with their friends. Malls all over the US were updating and expanding. The Mall of America was home to 350 stores, food courts, an amusement park, and other entertainment when it opened its doors.

Savvy Shopper Barbie, 1994

Nineties clothing trends were unique. Some young people dressed in preppy styles like Cher from the movie *Clueless*. Cher often wore plaid skirts, collared shirts, sweaters, and high socks. Back-to-School Barbie wore preppy clothes. Her big hair also matched the early '90s style.

Back-to-School Barbie, 1992

A mini magazine featuring the Generation Girl Collection, 1999.

The late '90s brought more friends for Barbie! Share a Smile Becky came out in 1996. She was the first doll to be sold with a wheelchair. Becky sold out within two weeks. In 1999, the Generation Girl collection of Barbie and friends was released. Chelsie, Ana, Lara, Tori, and Nichelle were added to store shelves. They were unique from each other in their backgrounds, personalities, and styles.

Share a Smile Becky, 1996

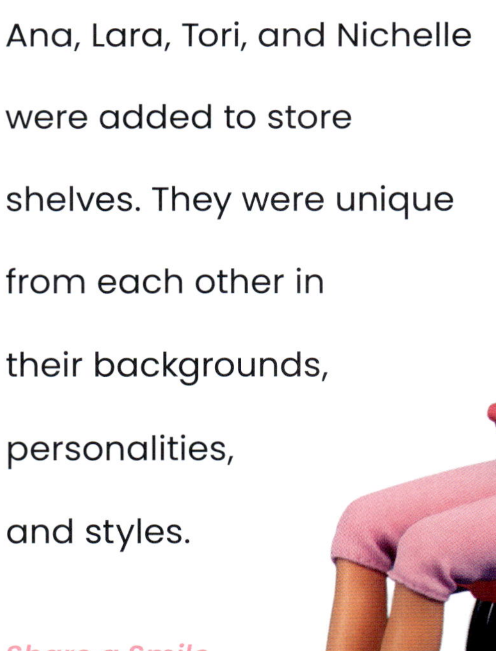

Mattel worked hard to keep new Barbies exciting and fun for kids to play with and use their imaginations. Barbies of the '90s came with never-before-seen **gimmicks**. Earring Magic Barbie and Ken came with accessories that kids could wear. Cool Blue Barbie came with hair paint. Children could use it in their own hair too! Beyond Pink Barbie came with a music cassette and glow-in-the-dark guitar.

Earring Magic Ken, 1993

Cool Blue
Barbie, 1998

Beyond Pink
Barbie, 1998

Big Steps for Barbie

Handler always hoped Barbie would inspire children to dream big about their futures. During the "Year of the Woman," Mattel worked hard so that Barbie continued to inspire modern women. In the first half of the nineties, Barbie took on careers that were usually dominated by men.

DID YOU KNOW?

There have been seven Presidential Candidate Barbies!

In 1992, Mattel released the first President Barbie. She came wearing a gown for the **inaugural** ball and a red suit. Barbie also became an officer in the Navy and a fighter pilot in the Air Force. Firefighter and Police Officer Barbie were released in the '90s as well.

Working Woman Barbie was released in 1999. Barbie had already been a high powered businesswoman in earlier decades. But Working Woman Barbie came with a bag, laptop, phone, coffee, and magazine. She was also packaged with a CD computer program that kids could use to build their own **letterhead**. Children could imagine their own successful futures.

Working Woman Barbie, 1999

Mattel released several Barbies celebrating the success of women's sports in the '90s. WNBA Barbie was released in 1998. Soccer Barbie came out the same year to honor professional soccer player Mia Hamm. Olympic Barbies included gymnasts and figure skaters.

As science and technology advanced, so did Mattel's products. The first Barbie computer game was released in 1996. Children could put together videos featuring Barbie and friends with music, voice-overs, and special effects. Mattel has continued to release video games ever since!

Ocean Friends Barbie and Baby Keiko were inspired by the 1993 film Free Willy. The toy collection also included Kira, Ken, a seal, and a dolphin.

The real life orca, Keiko, played Willy in *Free Willy*. In the film, Willy is freed from **captivity** with the help of his human friends. The '90s film brought attention to problems that happen when wild animals are held captive. Keiko was eventually released into the wild too! Barbie and Keiko helped kids learn and care about ocean animals.

Barbie advanced and changed as the world became more digital in the 1990s. Mattel was finding new and creative ways to inspire children. The next decade would be even bigger and better!

Olympic Skater Barbie and Ken, 1997. Barbie could spin on her own or in Ken's arms.

Making Connections

TEXT-TO-SELF

Have you ever played with Barbie or her friends?

If so, what kind of life did you imagine for them?

If not, what kind of life would you imagine?

TEXT-TO-TEXT

Have you read any books about other toys?

What did those toys have in common with

Barbie? How were they different?

TEXT-TO-WORLD

The 1990s brought lots of new technology. With

the help of an adult, research an invention

such as the Internet, cell phone, or personal

computer. Write a few sentences about what

you learned.

Glossary

captivity — the state of being held somewhere without the ability to leave.

Congress — the chief lawmaking body of the United States. It is made up of the Senate and the House of Representatives.

gimmick — a trick or device intended to attract attention.

homemaking — caring for a household by cooking, cleaning, and raising children.

inaugural — marking the beginning of an institution, activity, or period of office.

letterhead — stationery printed or engraved usually with a name and address.

prosperous — marked by financial success.

suburbs — areas or communities located just outside a city or town.

styling — to select and arrange clothing, hair, and makeup to create a particular fashion look.

trend — a current style or preference especially concerning clothing.

Index

Back-to-School Barbie, 18

Barbie Learns to Cook, 9

Beyond Pink Barbie, 20

careers, 8, 10, 22, 24–25

Cool Blue Barbie, 20

dreamhouse, 8

Earring Magic Barbie and Ken, 20

Free Willy, 28

Generation Girl collection, 19

Handler, Ruth, 6, 8–9, 22

malls, 17

Mattel, 6–8, 20, 22, 24, 26–27, 29

Ocean Friends Barbie, 28

original Barbie, 4, 7, 9

Presidential Candidate Barbie, 24

Share a Smile Becky, 19

sports, 15, 26

Suburban Shopper Barbie, 9

technology, 14, 27

Totally Hair Barbie, 16

women, 10, 12–13, 22

Working Woman Barbie, 25

Year of the Woman, 12–13, 22

DiscoverRoo! ONLINE RESOURCES

This book is filled with videos, puzzles, games, and more! Scan the QR codes* while you read, or visit the website below to make this book pop.

popbooksonline.com/nineties

*Scanning QR codes requires a web-enabled smart device with a QR code reader app and a camera.